I0180855

Transnational Activism Networks and Gendered Gatekeeping

Negotiating Gender in an African Association of Informal Workers

Ilda Lindell

NORDISKA AFRIKAINSTITUTET, UPPSALA 2011

INDEXING TERMS:
Informal sector
Social movements
International organizations
Grass roots groups
Networks
Associations
Women's organizations
Women's participation
Leadership
Gender relations
Feminism
Case studies
Mozambique

The opinions expressed in this volume are those of the author
and do not necessarily reflect the views of the Nordiska Afrikainstitutet.

ISSN 0280-2171
ISBN 978-91-7106-712-8
Language checking: Peter Colenbrander
© The author and Nordiska Afrikainstitutet 2011
Production: Byrå4
Print on demand. Lightning Source UK Ltd.

Contents

Acknowledgements

The author wishes to thank the Swedish International Development Cooperation Agency, Department of Research Cooperation, for financial support for this project. Thank you to all the interviewees who were willing to share their views and experiences. The author is also grateful for the insightful comments of three anonymous peer-reviewers. Thank you also to Peter Colenbrander for assistance with language editing.

A shorter version of this paper has been published in the journal *Global Networks*, 11:2, pp. 222–241.

Abstract

The paper explores emerging transnational networks of organized informal workers, with empirical reference to a local association based in Mozambique and a transnational network of which it is part. It uncovers the gendered spatialities of this transnational activism, how participation is unequal and heavily mediated rather than direct, and how influential actors engage in practices of gate-keeping and boundary-making that keep some actors in place. The paper explores the tensions that emerged as a result of the divergent gender ideologies espoused by different participant actors. The struggles and contestations that arise from this transnationalism, it is argued, take the form of a politics that is multidirectional, multi-sited and thoroughly gendered. The paper attempts to move beyond the current polarization of the debate that tends to oppose scalar and network perspectives on spatial politics in the global age, and applies theoretical work that problematizes the unequal and contested spatialities of transnational activism. Feminist scholarship further sheds light on the gendering processes at work in the transnationalization of a grassroots association.

Keywords: Transnational, gender relations, networks, associations, informal

The last few years have seen a rapid increase in the academic literature on transnational movements, part of a mounting interest in the sources of resistance to neoliberal globalization. Such literature highlights a wide range of movements and networks, which in turn reflect a great variety of concerns and constituencies. While many of these movements have been initiated in the North, some are driven by people from the Global South to contest various forms of destitution and assert a variety of basic economic and cultural rights. Such transnational organizing is also increasingly evident in Sub-Saharan Africa and an organization such as Shack Dwellers International for example connects people in a number of countries. Some of these transnational initiatives are particularly concerned with the growing numbers of people in the South depending on various forms of informal work.[1] This paper looks into the process of transnationalization of an association of informal workers based in Africa as it becomes involved in an international network of similar organizations. It will show that while this transnational engagement opens up new political possibilities, it also poses new challenges to participants, creates new contradictions and sets in motion new kinds of contestation. The paper discusses issues of exclusion, of boundary construction, practices of mediation and of gendered gate-keeping and the struggles involved. It uncovers the tensions that emerge from divergent gender ideologies within a transnational network.

The paper draws on seemingly opposed theoretical perspectives on spatial politics in the global age, to interrogate the spatialities of this transnational activism. On the one hand, debates centred around notions of geographical scale bring to the fore the differential possibilities of different social actors to transnationalize or re-scale their activities. On the other hand, network perspectives discard scalar boundaries and territorially based struggles to emphasize transnational networked forms of politics. The paper seeks to move beyond the polarization of the debate that opposes scalar and network perspectives, by drawing on the insights and critiques of both, with a view to apply a more nuanced, textured, spatially and socially differentiated understanding of transnational grassroots activism. By doing so, the paper situates itself in a new generation of studies that seeks to problematize the unequal and contested spatialities of such activism. The discussions are further enriched by insights from feminist critique and scholarship on power in transnational movements, on women's position within these movements and grassroots organisations, on the gendered work

1. By 'informal' is meant activities that are unprotected by written law and/or evade that law in some respect. 'Informal workers' are people making a living by engaging in such activities – including the self-employed.

of borders and boundaries, and on the perils of 'global sisterhood' ideals and of universal models for women's activism and empowerment.

Scales, Networks and the Contested Spatialities of Transnational Activism

In the last decade there have been new waves of theorizing interrogating the ways we understand spatial transformations associated with processes of "globalization". One strand of theorization of potential relevance for understanding contested processes of transnationalization of grassroots activism relates to a reconceptualization of geographical scale. Such reconceptualization has led to a shift from understanding scale as absolute and pre-given towards a notion of scale as socially constructed.[2] In this now large body of work, scales are viewed as constructed and reconstructed by social actors and as resulting from social processes. Such processes entail social and political struggle, as actors strive to exercise power or seek to restrain the power of others. Changes in the scalar reach of different social actors are seen as associated with changes in power relations and the strengthening of some actors and the disempowerment of others (Swyngedouw 1997, 2000, Uitermark 2002) – processes often referred to as "the politics of scale". From this perspective, the geographical scale of an actor's activities is understood as being both the outcome and the medium of struggles for power – an important insight for this paper. In this conception of scale, the capability to "re-scale" is often understood as being closely related to social power (Smith 1992, Swyngedouw 1997, 2000, Gough 2004). Some of the contributors refer to the notion of "power-geometries", initially proposed by Doreen Massey (1993, 1999) to highlight how different interests and groups differ in their ability to connect across space and how some actors are in a position to initiate and control global flows whereas others are at the receiving end.

However, while the above body of work has developed in a variety of directions, a greater part of it has tended to concentrate on the contemporary re-scaling of corporations and the nation-state and to focus on scalar reorganization as the outcome of the strategies and interests of hegemonic actors.[3] This reduces the field of vision to one particular contradiction or axis of analysis, in which the ability to "jump scales" is often assigned to capital, while labour (the poor), grassroots movements and resistance in general are assumed to be confined to the local level. Such interpretations failed to incorporate the abilities of social movements to re-scale and neglected other axes of differentiation at work in contemporary "power-geometries" – including those along gender

---

2. Smith (1992, 1993); Swyngedouw (1997, 2000); Delaney and Leitner (1997); Herod and Wright (2002).
3. See for example Smith (1993); Swyngedouw (1997); Brenner (1999); Uitermark (2002); Gough (2004). For a critique of these ideas, see for example Escobar (2001); Harcourt and Escobar (2005); Featherstone (2004:626, 2007); Featherstone et al. (2007).

and other lines. Some observers also consider that ascribing essential attributes to different scales and assigning agency to a particular spatial resolution (such as the "global" or the "local") is politically debilitating (Gibson-Graham 2002, Marston et al. 2005:427, Moore 2008).

Assumptions of this sort are in fact deeply entrenched in the research imaginary across a variety of fields. They are also visible in most analyses of the politics of informality, which tend to depict the agency of informal workers as necessarily entrapped in place (see, for example, Bayat 2004 and Cross 2007; and Lindell 2010 for a fuller discussion). Some feminist scholarship has also laid bare the gender-blind character of the above scale debates and pointed to the necessity of re-thinking scale from a gender perspective. McDowell (2001) challenges the common assumption in economic geography that "gender ... is significant only at the local scale" (p. 228) and stresses how gendered practices "construct particular cross-scalar relations" (p. 233) that have often been ignored. Conway (2008) and Masson (2006) also discuss how women's movements are involved in the construction of scale. The above fixation with the scalar strategies of powerful actors is associated with a conception of scales as being hierarchically ordered.[4] From this perspective, "the politics of scale is associated with vertical relations among nested territorially defined political entities" (Helga Leitner in Marston et al. 2005:417) and with establishing territories of control. In this hierarchical thinking, some argue, scales are treated as already existing and ontological categories (Moore 2008). They are conceived as spatial containers of social relations and as discrete and bounded areal units with fixed and identifiable boundaries (Amin 2002, 2004, Moore 2008:212, 216). This criticism has led to the development of more nuanced conceptions of scale, as discussed below.

Many analysts have instead proposed network readings of socio-spatial relations. Questioning notions of scale hierarchies and associated vertical relations, they propound instead a "flat ontology" of networks of horizontal social relations that span space (Marston et al. 2005). The emphasis is on the spatial extensiveness of relations that cut across multiple scales rather than being confined to a particular territory (Amin 2002, Featherstone 2004). Such interactions are viewed as multi-directional, non-linear and as connecting multiple "social sites" (Marston et al. 2005:427). Notions of rhizome and actor-networks have been used to challenge conceptions of discrete scales. Network approaches unsettle notions of fixed boundaries and of defined and bounded territories (Herod and Wright 2002, Amin 2002, 2004, Marston et al. 2005, Bulkeley 2005, Moore 2008). From that perspective, boundaries between scales are impossible to dis-

---

4. For such a conception, see for example Brenner (1998) and Smith (1993). For a critique, see among others, Amin (2002, 2004); Marston et al. (2005); Bulkeley (2005); Moore, (2008:209–10); McDowell (2001:230–233).

cern. Emphasis is instead placed on the boundlessness and the fluidity of spatial interactions.

Network concepts have become popular in the study of contemporary transnational activism. This trend reflects a common perception that in this global age territorially based struggles and place-bound politics are giving way to transnational networked forms of politics (for a discussion, see Featherstone 2007 and Cumbers et al. 2008). Such transnational networks are often understood in terms of deterritorialized social relations and as characterized by free flows across space of information, to which all participants have access (Hardt and Negri 2001, 2004; for a discussion see Cumbers et al. 2008:185). These transnational horizontal networks are frequently depicted as decentred and dispersed into "the multitude", as "ungoverned" as well as inclusive and participatory. Network perspectives have certainly broadened the understanding of politics beyond the confines of the "nation-state" and the "local", as well as brought to the fore the transnational activities of non-hegemonic actors (see for example, Featherstone 2004, 2008). These insights are thus of importance for the case presented in this paper. However, some of the criticism that has been directed at network perspectives is also of critical relevance for the argument pursued here.

Recent work has called for a deeper problematization of the spatialities of transnational activism, by paying closer attention to the complex and contested geographies of transnational networks (Routledge 2003, 2008, Featherstone et al. 2007, Sidaway 2007, Cumbers et al. 2008). This paper can be situated in this emerging body of inquiry. Firstly, Routledge and Cumbers (2009:82–92), among others, assert the critical role of place in transnational networks – albeit discarding territorially bounded notions of place – to emphasize that "global justice networks" are constituted simultaneously by spatially extensive and territorially intensive relations (p. 86). Social movements participating in transnational networks, they argue, continue to be territorialized, i.e., grounded in territorially or place-based struggles (Routledge and Cumbers 2009:43). They are embedded in place-specific configurations of social relations and particular local histories, as well as local cultural and political contexts – an embeddedness that tends to be neglected in many network analyses (Escobar 2001, Routledge 2003, Cumbers et al. 2008:192, Conway 2008). Places thus shape actors' identities and particular meanings as well as their political claims and place-specific discourses (Routledge and Cumbers 2009:82–4). Secondly, highly diverse participant movements may also have divergent agendas, advocate different strategies or subscribe to diverging ideologies (Routledge 2003, Conway 2008). Such differences may generate tensions between movements in networks. And so may the above particularities of place – as is the case "where different place-specific understandings of gender relations operate, with highly patriarchial local social systems clash[ing] with more progressive forms" (Routledge and Cumbers 2009:87).

Thirdly, transnational networks may contain power relations and inequalities, manifested in the differential access to information, resources, mobility, etc. Routledge (2008) criticizes actor-network theory for insufficiently problematizing issues of power in transnational activist networks: "The causes of and accountability for differential power relations have been precluded, as have the productive dimensions of that power" (p. 199), i.e., that unequal relations may be challenged and contested. He insists that while power is dispersed throughout the network, it also becomes centred on particular nodes and actors. He exemplifies this through the role of "imagineers", key actors who "translate" the vision of the network to the grassroots and wield considerable influence. In similar vein, Featherstone (2007, 2008), while applying a network approach, also questions the notions of smooth space underlying much writing on transnational activism. His work brings to light instances of contested relations in transnational networks and of negotiated articulations between participant movements. It illustrates the exclusionary practices through which networks are constructed and how the "policing" of these networks ensured "the enrolment of particular kinds of activists" and shaped their contours (2007:447).

Finally, Cumbers et al. (2008:183, 195) state that "networks evolve unevenly over space" and that movements and actors within them vary in their ability to establish transnational connections. Furthermore, they argue, network discourses tend to reflect a "westernized, and elitist, vision of globalization" (p. 189). The ideas of fluidity and free access may apply to "middle class activists from the Global North ... but they are unlikely to apply to the majority of grassroots activists ... in the Global South" (p. 189). While there is no reason to generalize, such differences are of relevance for the analysis in this paper of the perils of transnational connection by an association of informal workers in an African setting. Indeed, many (though not all) informal workers in Africa lack material resources and sufficient literacy, have limited access to internet technologies and face multiple constraints on their mobility. Among them, women, often overrepresented at the lowest income levels, are potentially even more constrained. The ability of these groups to connect with transnational movements should thus not be taken for granted. On the other hand, when they (or some of them) succeed, this should be considered a substantial achievement with potential political effects (Lindell 2010).

Some of the above dimensions of the contested nature of transnational activism have also come to the fore in a parallel debate on transnational feminist movements. In this debate, there is increasing emphasis on the local embeddedness of such movements and on the importance of the cultural and political contexts from which they emerge (Basu 1995, Naples 2002a, Miles 2004, Lyons 2004). Power relations in women's "global movements" have also been intensely debated. Much of the discussion has focused on the inequalities between women in the North and the South in terms of who is able to set the agenda, define the issues and determine the modalities of action (Basu 1995, Naples 2002a, b, Miles 2004, Conway 2008). These inequalities are seen as a form of cultural hegemony and as a source of considerable division and tension among women in transnational movements. Some feminist writers have also emphasized from a gender perspective the importance of borders and boundaries in relation to the international and the transnational. Pettman (1996) discusses the power and the violence that are deployed to maintain such borders and keep women "in place" and away from international politics. Mohanty (2006:2) promotes a transnational feminism that is "attentive to borders" (of various kinds) and to the "containment that borders represent", while at the same time stressing "the emancipatory potential of crossing" such borders. These insights from feminist debates are of relevance for wider discussions about the complex spatialities of transnational activism more generally.

While there is considerable academic work on transnational feminist movements as part of a feminist critique of global restructuring (see also Hale and Wills 2007, Hawkesworth 2006, Conway 2008), the growing anti-globalization movements of the last decade have been scarcely scrutinized through a gender lens, even though considerable numbers of women participate in them. Some feminist scholars have noted that such movements tend to marginalize feminist struggles (Mohanty 2006:249–50, Conway 2008:8). Likewise, there is growing criticism of much of the anti-globalization literature for being "ungendered" and masculinist, reflecting a long tradition of gender-neutral International Relations research (Marchand 2005, Amoore 2005:209, Mohanty 2006:249-50). In this literature, women and their struggles tend to be rendered invisible. This is so even though earlier feminist scholarship showed the thoroughly gendered nature of civil societies and social movements in general, i.e., that they are permeated by unequal gender relations and male domination (Petersson and Runyan 2005, Hawkesworth 2006:102). Women's participation in dual-sex social movements does not necessarily end their oppression as women nor mean that women enjoy equal influence with men in such movements – as has been noted for instance in the case of many male-dominated trade unions (Petersson and Runyan 2005). There are thus good reasons to look into gender power relations (as well as into their contestation) within transnational activist networks.

Beyond the polarized debate on scales vs. networks

Scalar and network perspectives have come to be seen as opposed interpretations of spatial politics in this global age. Some writers, however, see this polarization as exaggerated and unproductive and see common analytical ground between the two perspectives (McDowell 2001:230–3, 239, Bulkeley 2005, Moore 2008). More flexible conceptions of scale posit scale as relational and fluid and discard clear-cut boundaries between different scales (Howitt 2003) – while others have realized that networks have boundaries too (Bulkele 2005), as well as their own power geometries (Routledge 2008). Boundaries between scales are instead viewed as porous, blurred and shifting. Rather than fixed, they are constructed and contested by social actors. Reifying and essentializing notions of scale as spatial resolutions that pre-exist social action are replaced by a concern with "scalar practices" and with "varying degrees of scaleness" to stress that scales are contingent upon social practices (Moore 2008:218). These alternative conceptualizations of scale – which are adopted in this paper – come close to network accounts of spatiality concerned with the geographies "produced through practices and relations of different spatial reach and duration" (Amin 2002:389). Similarly, Routledge and Cumbers (2009:43), in their conception of "global justice networks", see "different geographical scales ... [as] links of various lengths in networks". Scale politics, which they see as a key feature of such networks, refers to "the uneven scaling of political opportunities" that effects "the geographical strategies ... of social movements ... and political elites" (p. 79–80). Finally, transnational activism networks may operate through both horizontal connections (i.e., decentred, mutual benefit) and vertical or hierarchical relations (i.e., with identifiable "centres" of power from which an ideological vision and a political programme emanate). Not seldom, these two supposedly opposing logics are used in combination, and thus become blurred in practice (Juris 2004, Routledge and Cumbers 2009, chapter 3).

This paper draws on the insights from both flexible understandings of scale and from the more spatially and socially sensitive view of networks discussed above, while rejecting problematic assumptions in both perspectives. The paper questions both the scale perspective that sees non-hegemonic actors as necessarily entrapped in place and denies them agency, and network perspectives that assume unrestrained mobility and access and render invisible the power relations in networks. It contests polarized views of politics that focus on either bounded spaces and place-bound struggles or on boundary-less transnational networks. Instead, the paper stresses the multiple and complex spatialities of resistance. It shows how popular actors are able to network transnationally, but how they are not equally able to do so. It argues that for those less able to connect beyond their local settings, boundaries do matter. This makes relevant the study not only of how connections are fostered in transnational activism – the usual focus of attention in network perspectives – but also how disconnections are sustained. It calls for a situated analysis of the power struggles involved in the production and contestation of these boundaries and in the continuous reconfiguring of transnational networks.

The paper addresses the processes of transnationalization of an organization of informal workers based in Mozambique, through its engagement in a transnational activist network and illustrates how these processes are both differential and contested. It explores the politics that arise from this widening connectivity, in particular the tensions and contradictions over gender issues that emerged among multiple actors and at several points or "sites" of interaction. It illustrates how unequal gender relations within a dual-sex association, shaped by and embedded in a specific local context, came into conflict with the gender ideologies espoused by other actors in the transnational network of which the association is part. A "power geometry" comes to light in which differential participation in international activities is structured along gender lines. This is partly the result of practices of "gendered gate-keeping" that have sometimes worked to the disadvantage of women. The paper shows how, in a context such as the one being examined, participation in the studied transnational activist network, rather than being free and inclusive, is restricted and heavily mediated by actors who command considerable power. It discusses the tensions and struggles that arise from the above-mentioned inequalities, practices and ideological divergences related to the connections and disconnections of transnational organizing. What emerges is a *different* politics of scale from the kind proposed by conventional scale models, and one that is thoroughly gendered.

The empirical part of the paper is based on varied sets of empirical data. The first set results from a field study of a vendors' association in Maputo, Mozambique. It consists of interviews with 23 persons in leadership positions in the association and about 25 vendors operating in market places affiliated with the association. The views of a few state officials and of a local politician were also recorded. The second set of data pertains to the global network of vendors of which the association is part. A person in a leading position in the global network was interviewed on several occasions. A group discussion was held with representatives of a South African group, another member of the network and one with which the association in Maputo had undertaken exchanges. Research methods also included participant observation, such as attending an international conference of African organizations of informal workers. The names of organizations involved are omitted, and fictitious names are used in quoting interviewees, in order to protect their anonymity.

I conducted most of the interviews in Portuguese, and a translator was very seldom necessary. Direct conversations without the mediation of a translator, in a language which most respondents were acquainted with, made it easier to establish initial contact with them and to conduct the interviews in an informal and friendly atmosphere. Yet respondents were sometimes very cautious about certain sensitive topics, including gender relations within the association. In some cases, women vendors might have feared my judgment of their views on gender issues, and may have worried about how I would portray their association and about endangering its reputation. Indeed, as a European female researcher

I had to confront some of my own assumptions and values and interrogate my own privilege to define, for example, what are the legitimate agendas, strategies and forms of struggle for organized women or informal workers in Maputo – a discussion that surfaces again later in this paper. As others have noted before, it is important to be aware of "the power which comes from the [researcher's] ability to orientalize, ethnicize, racialize or sexualize members of other nations or groups" (Mackie 2001:182). Acknowledging the dangers of "The gaze of powerful observers on those less powerful" (p. 183) is critical in a study like this one, where a researcher based in a privileged country writes about African realities and the concerns of (less privileged) African men and women. Being an outsider to Mozambican society, I cannot claim to comprehend fully the realities and motivations of the interviewed men and women, given our very different histories and locations. My interpretations and representations of them might be limited or even distorted, which is hopefully compensated for by allowing respondents to speak for themselves to the extent that this is possible. My sympathy for the cause of the involved organizations may also influence my judgments.

The empirical section begins with a presentation of the international network and of its gender policy. This is followed by a presentation of the studied association, including its internal gender hierarchy. The paper then discusses the tensions over gender issues that arose from the international exchanges.

The international network grew out of a realization of the limitations of organizing at the local level and of the need for organizing internationally, given the global scope of informalization processes. The launch of the international organization occurred in 2002. It was preceded by a series of international meetings and workshops that gathered representatives of associations from different countries and regions with the aim of getting views and input that would steer the drafting of the constitution of the organization and its policy on a number of issues.

The activities of the international organization include representing the interests of informal workers in international forums (such as the International Labour Organization), organizing international conferences for representatives of groups of informal workers, and arranging exchange visits between affiliated groups. Representatives of the studied local association have participated in such conferences and exchange visits. The network has, at the time of writing, some 30 member organizations across regions of the Global South, although organizations in Africa have been more heavily represented. It is composed of membership-based organizations that organize informal workers in their respective countries. Its affiliates include a wide range of groups, encompassing both organizations originating in the informal economy and trade unions that organize informal workers. Both women's groups and mixed groups are represented in the network. While a number of the latter have men as leaders, some of the women's groups appear to be quite influential in the network, as is the case with a large women's organization based in India. Most member groups appear to have an urban rather than rural basis. The stated target group of the network is the poorest workers in the informal economy, with particular concern being expressed for women.

The structure of the international organization encompasses an international council, which is responsible for, among other things, planning and monitoring the activities of the organization. The council is composed of representatives who are elected from among member organizations, and of an international president and other office bearers. The international congress, which is to be held at least once every three years, gathers a number of delegates from each member organization on the basis of membership size. The congress is the occasion for discussing and adopting resolutions and policies put forward by members of the international council or by member organizations. All of the above positions are elective.

Resembling something between a federation and a network of organizations, what I will often refer to as "the network", is characterized by a mix of horizontal and vertical relations, rather like certain other transnational networks (see

Juris 2004, Routledge and Cumbers 2009). On the one hand, its structure is partly similar to that of trade unions, with governing bodies and "vertical relationships of representation and delegation" (Routledge and Cumbers 2009:50), and with representatives of the various member organizations making up the leadership body. On the other hand, horizontal relations for mutual benefit between member organizations, such as exchange visits, are one of the important benefits of affiliation. Member organizations also retain their autonomy in the running of their internal affairs, rather than being forced to follow a strict political programme and strategy designed and delivered by a vanguard international leadership.

The network qualifies as what Batliwala (2002) calls "grassroots movements", which differ from many global advocacy networks and Non-Governmental Organizations (NGOs), in that the former have "structured links" with grassroots constituencies (p. 397), thus "enjoy[ing] high levels of legitimacy and right to representation" (p. 404) and potentially being more accountable to their constituencies and able to derive their priorities and agendas from grassroots organizations in more bottom-up ways (p. 408). Furthermore, the network was initiated in the South and has an explicit South bias, for example by developing structures that ensure that its leadership is drawn from organizations in the South. The network thus tries to avoid the North-South inequalities that have characterized many transnational movements. Moreover, even if it has succeeded in attracting funding from the North, the network's commitment to the concerns of vulnerable informal workers remains.

However, other kinds of asymmetries may develop, although further empirical work would be needed to describe their evolving contours. There are great variations in the size of member groups and, since the number of delegates each organization can send to the international congress is proportionate to its membership, large organizations will be better represented at the congress and potentially have an advantage in terms of influencing decisions. Moreover, representatives from countries such as South Africa, India, Zambia and Ghana, who were among the founding members, seemed for this and other reasons to be well positioned to influence the orientation of the network. While many member organizations depend completely on modest membership fees, a few may be better resourced and able to attract international funding. Having such a broad geographical reach, the network encompasses many different languages, always a challenge in such networks (see Mackie 2002:196). Most of the founder groups, for example, are fluent in English and may enjoy an advantage in debates within the network. Member organizations may also vary in their competence in and access to internet technologies, which in itself can make for power inequalities in a network (Routledge and Cumbers 2009:55). These asymmetries raise questions about free flows of information and smooth space in network perspectives.

On the basis of the internal documents of the international organization and of interviews with leading persons in and representatives of member groups, it is possible to provide the basic contours of its policy on gender issues. The constitution lays out compulsory gender quotas for the bodies of the organization. At least half of the international office bearers must be women. Of the eleven representatives of member organizations on the international council, at least six must be women. Accordingly, a stipulated share of the delegates representing each member organization at the international congress must be women. The organization generally requires that 50 per cent of participants be women in activities sponsored by it but carried out by affiliates.

The explicit concern of the organization with women is also evident in other ways. Its constitution states that one of its primary aims is "to build and strengthen the capacity and leadership of women' vendors. The fact that the organization was from the outset inspired by a large and influential women's union in India certainly contributed to the early taking of a position on gender issues. Indeed, the organization adopted a gender policy at its launch meeting in 2002. This policy acknowledges that women constitute the majority of street vendors in most countries and are often overrepresented among the poorest groups of vendors. It expresses the commitment of the organization to "empowering women", as well as to building leadership particularly among women. Two other policy resolutions adopted later by the international congress reiterate these intents. In these documents the organization commits itself to promoting the economic and social rights of women informal workers and the value of their work, as well as to working to reverse the subordinate status usually ascribed to women and to uphold relations of equality between women and men. Member organizations are advised to involve women in all their programmes and to develop equitable and democratic practices, including the participation of women in decision-making and representation activities. In the words of one of the international leaders speaking at an activist conference I attended, "women's empowerment is a big issue for us. We want to empower women to become negotiators and leaders".

Gender equity thus constitutes a core principle of the organization. These goals, however, are not easy to attain. As an interviewed leader explained, one of the main challenges arises from the fact that many member organizations are dual-sex groups with male leaders and largely female constituencies. "In international meetings", the interviewee added, "virtually everyone verbally subscribes to notions of gender equality and of social justice". Male leaders may even pay lip service to the gender policy of the network and use a progressive gender discourse in order to minimize confrontation, while at the same time they may engage in discriminatory gender practices. The international organization tries to deal with these gender contradictions by instituting mechanisms, such as the gender quotas described above, to secure a fair representation of women. However, its leaders avoid dictating to individual organizations how to deal with gender hierarchies within their own organizations as, in their view, this is something that cannot be imposed from without.

The share of the population of Maputo depending on informal activities for an income has been growing rapidly (Lachartre 2000, Lundin 2001). Given the scarcity of formal jobs, a variety of groups, including redundant workers, rural migrants and demobilized soldiers, try to make a living in the urban informal economy. One of the most visible manifestations of this is the growth of unplanned market places and the proliferation of street vending activities in the city. These developments are generally disliked by local authorities, who look upon them as disfiguring the city. Vendors are frequently harassed and unplanned market places, considered illegal, are often threatened with demolition. An association of market vendors was created in 1999, mainly as a response to this hostility.

The association expanded rapidly and became a city-wide organization, with representation in a number of market places in Maputo. At the time of my fieldwork, it was composed of an executive committee as well as a number of market committees in the city (a total of 15 at that time). The members of both are elected and all persons in leadership positions originate in, and derive their livelihoods from, the city markets. The market committees regulate access to selling sites, organize cleaning and provide infrastructure and security, with fees collected in their respective markets. The committees enjoy substantial authority within their markets and are the only entities which de facto manage the markets and regulate relations within them – though they differ in their management styles.

A women's department was established in the association soon after its creation. It has an elected coordinator who supervises the work at the city-wide level as well as elected representatives – all of them women – in affiliated market places. The activities of the women's department include conducting meetings in the markets, organizing recreational activities, regulating conflicts in the markets and setting the rules of conduct for women vendors. Each affiliated market place thus has both a market committee and a women's department, and both are supposed to collaborate and coordinate activities, as explained by one of the women leaders. Representatives of both structures are entitled to participate in weekly meetings at the headquarters of the association, where they have the opportunity to voice the concerns of vendors in their respective markets.

The association is membership-based. Its constituency is diverse, including men and women, various ethnic groups, employers and employees and vendors of varying economic capacity, ranging from those selling a bucket of local vegetables to those retailing larger stocks of higher value imported foodstuffs. However, most were small-scale low-income vendors, reflecting the general income structure of informal vending in Maputo (see Lundin 2001). The association itself is very modestly resourced, as it relies on a predominantly impoverished constituency, modest contributions from affiliated markets and no major external funding. It is housed in humble, poorly maintained premises, with simple furniture and no computer equipment.

Relations within the association have gone through periods of upheaval. Some of the conflicts have been between persons in leadership positions on the executive committee and in the markets, and have pertained to financial matters, access to posts and delayed elections. Relations between the headquarters and the rank-and-file also appeared to be somewhat top-down. Many of the interviewed vendors seemed poorly informed about the plans devised at the headquarters. On occasion, some vendors felt the association's leaders were too dilatory in coming to their aid when their livelihoods came under threat. On other occasions, however, the association has mobilized vendors across market places for large scale concerted action.

The association is the only force in the city speaking up for vulnerable informal income earners. Its main target is the municipal council, which was reluctant to accept the existence of the association and has attempted to disrupt it in various ways. Relations between the association and the municipal council have been complicated and conflicts have frequently occurred (Lindell 2008). However, the association's leadership maintains close links with the (formerly single) ruling party as a means of exerting pressure on less cooperative local government officials. In fact, some association and market committee leaders have or had (low-rank) positions in the party. They tend to engage in political campaigns in the markets in favour of the party, which has ruled at both central and city level since independence.

Interviews with members of the executive, with heads of market committees and representatives of the women's departments in a number of affiliated markets revealed how the association is structured by gender as well as various views concerning women's participation.

The discourse of the male leaders of the association makes reference to equality between men and women, to respect for female colleagues, etc. Many of the interviewed representatives of the women's department in the markets frequently depicted general satisfaction with the existing conditions for women's participation in the association. They stated their opinions were heard at the weekly meetings at headquarters and that they participated in decision-making, as they had an equal vote with men. According to their accounts, they were usually invited by the male leadership to participate in meetings with the city council. Women vendors usually considered that the association leaders defended them well against the city council. Generally, respondents seemed keen to give a positive picture of the association.

Upon closer scrutiny, however, a more complicated picture emerges. To begin with, there is a clear gender hierarchy within the association. While the constituency of the association is largely female, as reported by the association leaders themselves the leadership was predominantly male. This was evident both in the executive committee and in the market committees: among the latter, only three of 15 committees were headed by women. Women's access to leadership positions was mainly restricted to posts within the women's department. The male leaders interviewed often explained this state of affairs by referring to women's lack of will, self-interest or to their lack of ability to exercise leadership, as exemplified by the following quote. Samuel is a member of the committee in charge of market A, one the biggest in Maputo, and an energetic and charismatic man, who seems able to mobilize the vendors for many activities in the market. He explained, "Women in a society like this ... women have no talent for domination ... sometimes when you give a post to a woman, she says she is a child, that she doesn't know anything. Then you're already vulnerable as a structure". The views of certain of the women interviewees resonated with some of these ideas. For example, Manuela, a woman with a leadership position within the association, puts it this way, "Our Mozambican custom is still to give one's place to a man. When the women want to make their own decisions and become leaders, they gain fear. We work together with them [men] but we lack the courage to be leaders". Another woman, Liliana, who leads the committee in market B and who enjoys a reasonable economic standing, also explained, "Women are afraid of competing [for leadership]. We've had in our minds that it is men that have to be in the front of everything, at home, at work", although she added, "this is changing".

Manuela further noted that there was a time when there were many complaints by women's department representatives in the markets about being ignored or by-passed by the male heads of the market committees, who at times even boycotted their work, withheld information and calls for meetings, etc. "The men are not understanding what the women's department is", she said. She continued:

> The women representing the women's department in the markets have as much competence as the men heading market committees ... We want the men to understand that we are equal ... This is the nightmare we're having, that men still ignore this ... We're still educating the heads of market committees to understand this [to collaborate with the women's department], but it's not easy. This is something new ... Men in leadership tend to steal the power from the women. If women are not active, they'll stay at the feet of the men in this institution. That's why we need strong women, who are not afraid, who can say openly what they do not want.

The women's department appears to remain a subaltern structure within the association. For instance, interviews with women in positions at different levels of the women's department revealed that the department is not entitled to a share of the (albeit meagre) resources of the association and enjoys little independence from its leaders concerning its own activities. The department's coordinator must, for example, first inform the president before conducting any activities with the women in the markets. In interviews with women with leadership positions at various levels of the association, it became evident that they were well aware of male dominance in the association. For example, one of the few female heads of market committees stated that "our wish is that all market committees would be headed by women". This awareness would grow into unrest during interactions with international partners, as will be discussed below.

Several constraints help to explain why women are barely represented in leadership positions in the association, even if these are elective. As mentioned above, women expressed fears about taking on such positions, with the result that most of those who volunteer as candidates are men. This lack of self-confidence may partly relate to the generally low levels of literacy among women. Moreover, many of the women vendors earn low incomes and thus cannot spare the time for association work. Typically, association and market committee leaders were relatively better off and could employ others to tend their businesses, leaving them time for associational activities. Several women vendors also pointed to their multiple responsibilities, both as breadwinners and in bearing the brunt of the reproductive work in the household. Others explained their husbands might oppose them in spending time on associational work: they would not allow their wives to spend all day at the market only to return home without an income. This attitude is to be understood in the context of a predominant configuration of gender relations in which men have traditionally been the income earners and women the housewives or farmers. In recent decades, men have increasingly had to accept the need for women to earn an income at the markets to compensate for their own lost ability to provide sufficient income for their households. The wider political environment may also discourage women from taking up "public roles", particularly the authoritarian governance style of local authorities and the narrow opportunities for civil society participation.

From the position of a Western researcher, it would be all too easy to represent women members as merely subordinate and as lacking agency – as Eurocentric writings have often done about women in the South (Basu 1995:2, Mackie 2001). Rather, the interviewed women were well aware of the gender hierarchy in the association and were consciously weighing their options, as will be discussed below. Through the women's department, they also created their own spaces: for example, they had their own discussions at women's meetings and developed solidarity through recreational activities and financial assistance to colleagues in difficulty. In addition, leaders of women's departments in the markets participated in meetings at the association headquarters as well as in meetings with city council officials, which may have provided opportunities for them to enhance their leadership capabilities.

The Mozambican association initiated its engagement with the international network in 2001 by attending an international meeting in Zambia. After that, the association participated in several international conferences and in exchange visits facilitated by the network. The interviewed individuals in the association who had participated in such activities expressed great appreciation of these international experiences. The latter created opportunities for expressions of solidarity between member groups – as exemplified below. The Mozambican participants also explained that they learned how informal workers in other countries and continents dealt with similar challenges. The knowledge of struggles and achievements in other places assisted them in their own local struggles with the municipal council and in articulating alternative visions for their city.

The association faces a range of constraints in its participation in the international network. While this is a multilingual network, English is a key language of communication and is foreign to virtually the entire leadership of the association, and even more so to its members. Dependence on language translation potentially slows down communication flows and hampers Mozambican participation in discussions at international events and in internet exchanges. Information flows are thus mediated rather than direct, and filtered through translation, if and when this is available and affordable. Distortions in translation, misunderstandings and gaps in information flows may in themselves generate tensions. Lack of computers and access to internet technologies in the association further impairs smooth information flows. These difficulties are not uncommon to many associations in Africa and the South, and women members are probably even more disadvantaged in this regard (see Mackie 2001:197 and Routledge and Cumbers 2009:55). These challenges seem to place the association on the periphery of the network and at the receiving end of key ideas.

The generally poor material circumstances of the association and of the majority of its members also constrain international mobility. Perhaps partly as a result of material constraints, mobility was restricted to individuals in various leadership positions. Local configurations of gender relations would add an additional twist to these unequal patterns of transnational participation.

Gendered gate-keeping

Participation by the association in the activities of the international network has not been pain free. One of the main sources of contention pertains to women's participation in international activities. The leadership of the association is aware of the gender policy of the international organization and that gender equity is one of its key concerns. According to the interviewed representatives of the network, these issues were discussed many times, and during such discussions the association leaders always gave the assurance that they respected the women and acknowledged that "women are the backbone of the organization". However, women were usually absent from the initial international exchanges. The leadership of the association appears to have engaged in gate-keeping, to the disadvantage of women. A number of examples drawn from the history of the international interactions of the association attest to this.

After its first attendance at an international meeting, the association was again invited to participate in a regional workshop in 2002 but declined to send any delegates, according to the network leaders interviewed. The latter sought an explanation from the association, without ever receiving one. In their view, the reason was that the association's leader was on an exchange visit and unwilling to allow others to represent the association abroad in his absence. In particular, they stated there seemed to be reluctance to allow women to participate in international activities. Consequently, the network's leadership began insisting on women's participation in such activities. For example, they reported that when the network facilitated an exchange visit to South Africa in 2002, it required that two or three of the five persons in the delegation be women. The association complied. Reportedly, however, a major split developed within the delegation, partly for reasons discussed below.

Later that year, the network held its launch conference. According to its leaders, the association was invited to send one delegate to the meeting, preferably a woman, in accordance with the established gender quotas aimed at ensuring a reasonable share of women participants. The invitation was in fact addressed to the head of the women's department in the association, they explained. The leaders of the association, however, nominated a different woman to attend, and also suggested that a second woman would participate. However, neither woman attended the launch meeting. By this time, the leaders of the network realized that some resentment related to gender issues had developed in the association.

On another occasion, the association did propose a woman as its candidate for election to the international council, the leaders of the network explained. She attended a couple of meetings but then failed to attend the international conference where the election was to take place, they reported. Network leaders tried to investigate the reasons and found that there was a conflict over who should participate in international activities. In particular, the head of the women's department at the time – described by some as an ambitious woman leader – was feeling sidelined. When the team to travel to South Africa was selected, she was again ignored, as revealed by a member of the delegation, and a different woman was chosen, leading to resentment between the women. It appears that some of the male leaders of the association were acting as gate-keepers, carefully selecting whom they wanted to send abroad. In the process, women were turned against each other. These tensions between women in leadership positions surfaced during the interviews conducted with them.

Thus, while the association was internationalizing by networking across space, patterns of participation in international activities were highly skewed as such internationalization rested on a handful of individuals within the association. This observation resonates with other work that questions notions of unconstrained mobility, of undifferentiated access to transnational networks and of boundlessness, which are common in network approaches to transnational activism. As noted by Cumbers et al. (2008), restricted mobility is common to many grassroots associations in the Global South, given the many constraints facing them. In the case of a dual sex association described here, women appear to have sometimes been even more constrained in their mobility, at least partly because of gender hierarchies within the association. From a scale politics perspective, differences in social power between men and women might explain these gendered patterns of unequal participation in international activities. In addition, as male leaders in the association engage in practices of gendered gatekeeping, they actively create and maintain boundaries that potentially keep (certain) women "in place". Their positions as gate-keepers and as mediators between the grassroots and the network may further reinforce their power. This suggests the importance of considering how power becomes centred on certain actors in transnational activist networks and of going beyond the flat ontologies espoused by network perspectives. The power of mediators and gatekeepers does not always go unchecked, however. The next section discusses how considerable gender unrest arose within the association but also how views among women on how to deal with gender hierarchies sharply diverged in the context of exchange visits with a sister organization in the network.

Exchange visits and gender unrest

As mentioned above, the international organization facilitated exchange visits between the Mozambican association and a South African organization. For the first visit, a delegation from the Mozambican organization travelled to South Africa. Some months later it was the turn of the South Africans to visit the association and its affiliated markets in Maputo. Members of both delegations were interviewed, in Mozambique and South Africa respectively.

The aim of the exchange visits was reportedly for the two groups to learn from each other's experiences. The interviewed Mozambicans seemed to greatly value these exchange visits for strengthening their ability to negotiate with Maputo municipal council. Those who had travelled to South Africa were enthusiastic about the conditions provided for market vendors there as well as the collaboration that existed between the vendors' association and the authorities. They explained how they used this knowledge to clearly formulate their demands to the Maputo authorities. Joaquim, committee leader in charge of market C, a large wholesale market, explained: "We went there [to the city officials] when we came back [from South Africa] and told them all we had seen there, including that we entered the informal market by escalator, the cleanliness, all that the municipal government does for the vendors." Hosting the South Africans also offered the association some reinforcement in its strained relations with local authorities. During their visit to Maputo, the South African delegation had a meeting with the city mayor during which, according to respondents from both organizations, they were very vocal about the rights of informal workers and the obligations of the authorities towards them. In the view of the leaders of the Mozambican association, the pressure exerted by a foreign group made a difference (even if temporary) to the willingness of local authorities to negotiate. As Routledge and Cumbers (2009) stress, transnational grassroots activism is often closely related to place-based territorial struggles. In this case, exchange visits between grassroots organizations and the associated learning and expressions of solidarity illustrate the benefits that can derive from such horizontal relations. Indeed, Routledge and Cumbers remark, transnational networking may provide "discursive and material resources" for a territorial struggle (p. 92).

The South African delegation apparently made a strong impression on women vendors in Maputo during its visit there. The latter often referred to the way the South African women confronted the Maputo authorities, gave interviews in the media and had their own union. Luisa, the head of the women's department in market D, remarked: "They are strong! They have created many things by themselves, without depending on men". However, these encounters also caused some unrest within the Mozambican association, particularly over gender issues.

The counterpart South African association was a women's-only organization and known to have a progressive stance on gender. The interviewed South African delegation considered there were considerable gender inequalities within the Mozambican association. They reported that during their visit to Maputo they were not allowed to meet with the women alone and that, in their meetings with the Mozambicans, the women present remained silent. By their own account and on the basis of their written report on the exchange visit, the South African women were outspoken about gender equality issues in those meetings. They asked the leaders of the association about "women's rights" in the association, advised them to "give the women opportunity to open their own projects" and spoke of "the importance of women's organization". According to the interviewed South African representatives, during both exchange visits the Mozambican women expressed interest in forming a women's-only organization and, not knowing how to set about doing so, wanted their South African colleagues to assist them. According to the latter's report, the head of the women's department at the time stated that "they must organize women and form a women's union". These exchange visits apparently triggered tensions over gender issues within the association.

The leaders of the international network – who noted that it was important not to create divisions within or between local groups – declared they had become aware of this and tried to address the problem. One of them, while on a visit in Maputo, learned that the Mozambican association's leaders considered that the South African group and the international network were pushing the "gender equality agenda" too hard and that this was causing problems within the association. Another leader of the network decided to visit the association with the aim of evaluating the exchange visit and resolving the problem. According to this leader, the Mozambican leaders would only refer to the positive aspects of the exchange visit, praise the international network and its leaders and refused to even acknowledge the disagreements on gender issues. Apparently, the association's leaders were so keen to join the network that they did not want to jeopardize that opportunity by discussing gender hierarchies or women's access to leadership posts and participation in international activities. This was the occasion when the association handed in its membership application and became a full member of the network.

In spite of the impact of the exchange visit and of the turmoil it created, when I interviewed the women vendors in the markets some months after the visit had taken place, a picture of harmonious gender relations in the association was frequently conveyed to me. Furthermore, whatever ambitions there had been about creating a women's organization were played down. Some of the interviewed women leaders considered that there were advantages to having a women's-only organization, but that this was not feasible at present, as the following quotes illustrate. Women's lack of experience and courage to assume leadership was often referred to by the respondents. Luisa for instance, expressed the view that the women would be able to achieve more if they organized autonomously:

> We'd have our own ideas, to show the men that we're able to do something brilliant ... Women's interests don't get prioritized, our ideas stand a bit in the back ... Although we work together, we don't really get to be equal. We don't have our own funds, we don't have our own initiative [freedom] of having something made by ourselves [building something by ourselves] ... The South Africans told us, "If you had your own fund, we could help you with ideas, it would be easier to collaborate between us women only". They were very surprised to see us work side by side with men; we had a very encouraging discussion with them, a wonderful experience. [But] we told them "leave it alone, this is the way we work".

Cristina expressed similar views. She is an influential woman in her market (market E) and in the association and is assertive in the way she speaks. She also has an ambitious vision for the association and its women and has reasonable economic standing. In her view, there is advantage in having a women's-only or-ganization, "But the association was created jointly with men and in the markets we also work close to the men. It would be difficult because women still lack the experience [understanding] that they have the same rights as men, that they can do the same work as men, the idea of equality. Women still see themselves as inferior". Two others, among them Liliana, even expressed the view that having a separate women's association was neither necessary nor a good alternative for women vendors in Maputo. Liliana explained,

> There is no difference. Because the Mozambican woman has always worked side by side with men, during the armed struggle already, it's always been like that. That's why we don't feel so much difference ... The South Africans told us that they had only women [as members], this was new to us ... For them a mixed organization was something new. They asked us, "Why isn't the women's department independent from the men, the association?" We answered that it is not possible because the department was born from the association ... and we also feel good working side by side with men.

Manuela, who had had the opportunity to interact closely with the South Afri-cans, further explained:

> Our association defends the interests of women and those of men in the in-formal sector, because the two [men and women] do the same activities. The problems that women face in the informal sector are the same as men's. We're all there [in the markets] to earn our daily bread. So we think it is better to work together [in one association] ... They [the South Africans] have their own policy; we also have our own policy that educates women on how to consider men as their partners in all kinds of work. They're keeping men away from their association. I don't understand it.

These sorts of statement – "we work side by side with men, we share the same problems, we consider men as partners in all sorts of work" – would surface again in interviews with other women vendors. In fact, they seem to resonate with the rhetoric by the single party on 'gender equality' following independ-ence.

In the above discourse, gender-related divisions are downplayed whereas what men and women vendors have in common is emphasized – in this case, shared vulnerability in the face of a persistent external threat, the city council. From this perspective, men and women thus ought to mobilize together in this struggle against their common enemy and in their efforts for recognition as legitimate workers. This way of framing the "real issues at stake" may have been used as a way of calming the gender tensions within the association. Women's acquiescence in this view was perhaps the price they had to pay to keep up the appearance of a "united front" against that external threat. While women leaders were conscious of unequal gender relations in the association, it seems that the defence of their rights as vendors was given higher priority than openly contesting those gender relations. And indeed, for many it is survival that is at stake.

The above illustrates the contradictions that arose out of international exchanges and how negotiating membership in the international network was permeated by tensions over gender issues. These contradictions can be seen as a form of scale politics resulting from the internationalization of the association, as well as understood from a network perspective that is sensitive to the contested relations involved in transnational activism. As pointed out by Routledge (2003) and Conway (2008), tensions and contradictions of various kinds can be expected among highly diverse movements participating in transnational grassroots networks. Gender issues were not necessarily the only sources of tension at work in this case: the somewhat peripheral position of the Mozambican association in the network may, of course, lead to some resentment, and language difficulties, including constant dependence on translation, can cause misunderstandings and gaps in communication, if not conflicts. The other international partners involved also occasionally expressed unease at the unrealistic financial expectations the association had of the network, and at its political strategy of working closely with the ruling party. However, in the early stages of international engagement – when this study was carried out – contestation over gender issues seemed to be among the most prominent sources of tension.

While exchange visits were highly appreciated by the Mozambican association for providing opportunities for learning and for solidarity towards their local struggle, differences became evident between the involved organizations regarding gender ideologies and strategies. The "clash" emerged from the encounter between two different associations coming from very different political and cultural contexts: a South African women's association known for its radical feminist stance and a Mozambican dual-sex association in which women were perceived by the former as playing a rather passive role. For example, for the South African delegation, the only way forward was for women to organize on their own. By contrast, the interviewed Mozambican women appeared to be skeptical of this idea and considered that they would be better able to protect their livelihoods by organizing together with men. This reluctance to embrace feminist models from abroad is not unique. Basu (1995:6) discusses how women in some contexts "regard feminism with deep skepticism" and see it as "narrowly associated with a particular ideology, strategy and approach", one that "demands a total transformation of the social order" (p. 6, 7). In many cases, Basu states, feminism takes instead "an incremental, hidden form of subversion enacted to protect families and communities rather than to undermine them" (p. 7). This incremental route seems to be the one the Mozambican women leaders have opted for, one that they perceived would not jeopardize their struggles for economic survival.

More generally, in their struggles, women have often fought for a great range of issues through, or in alliance with, male-dominated organizations (for example, in broader nationalist, working class and other struggles), often driven by "a sense of shared oppression with other groups" (Basu 1995:10) – a sense repeatedly expressed by the Mozambican women. These struggles too, Basu argues, are important manifestations of women's activism (p. 19). Indeed, there are growing calls for acknowledging the great diversity of women's activism and agency, "the multitudinous ways women organize on behalf of themselves and their communities" (Naples 2002a:6, b:275, 278). Radical versions of feminism that posit gender as the principal form of oppression are increasingly challenged by the recognition that women's identities are multiple and shaped by various and intersecting axes of discrimination (Mackie 2001:181, Naples 2002a:10, Basu 1995:4). Consequently, women may in their situated struggles emphasize class, "race, ethnicity ... as much as gender" (Basu 1995:17), just as the Mozambican women appear to be doing. Through collaborations with men, women have sometimes achieved tangible benefits for themselves and their families. That said, there are considerable documented gains and advantages for women in organizing autonomously of men and defining their own priorities, as well as costs and dangers in organizing across the sexes (for a discussion, see Basu 1995:8-10, Mendez 2002 and Miles 2004:7). For Basu, irrespective of whether "women organize on their own or as members of larger groups" the critical issue is "whether women's activism responds to their own concerns or those of external actors", such as the state (p. 10). In addition, as Sylvia Tamale (2004) has put it, what is needed is a form of leadership that is transformational, that "serves both men and women, poor and rich, and the powerless and powerful. It is inclusive, participatory, and horizontal and is centrally informed by feminist values such as participation and collaboration, diversity and pluralism, inclusiveness..." (Miles 2004:10). These values are critical for dual-sex grassroots organizations, such as the Mozambican one studied here. For while the core work of the Mozambican association addressed some of the key concerns of its female members, namely the protection of their right to a livelihood, the association leadership had still to acknowledge and actively work on the gender disparities within the organization and to strengthen participatory practices more generally.

The women leaders' perception that it was best not to break away and create their own association was probably based on the weighing of various considerations, ranging from relations within households, to relations within the association, to their positions in the informal economy and in the wider political environment. Their choices ought to be understood in the context of the local realities in which these women live. These include configurations of gender relations that have historically ascribed to women a role in reproductive tasks and unremunerated work and to men the privilege of public representation; a local political context characterized by an authoritarian governance style and narrow space for civil society participation more generally, as well as by an incipient women's movement to lean on. These complexities seem to go against understandings of transnational networks as de-territorialized and support claims that transnational activism is grounded and embedded in place-specific conditions and social relations. In similar vein, work on women's movements increasingly stresses the importance of varying local cultural and political contexts and the ways in which women's transnational activism is locally situated and embedded within difference (Basu 1995:4, 20, Lyons 2004). When such differences in women's realities, experiences and strategies are ignored, and universalizing feminist views are imposed, tensions arise and transnational solidarity is endangered (see Naples 2002a, Miles 2004, Basu 1995).

This paper investigates the tensions and contradictions that arose in connection with the engagement of an organization of informal workers based in Africa with a transnational activist network. The findings speak to both scalar and network perspectives on spatial politics. Rather than adhering to the usual polarization of these perspectives, the paper draws on insights from both as well as from their respective critiques to illustrate some dimensions of the multiple and complex spatialities involved. The empirical case is an illustration of spatially extensive relationships that connected grassroots organizations across space, while remaining closely tied to an ongoing territorial and place-based struggle (Routledge and Cumbers 2009:43), that between the Maputo association and the local authorities. Both horizontal connections (i.e., between the two grassroots associations) and a degree of vertical relations (i.e., between member groups and the leadership of the network) also seem to be at work, suggesting the "entangled operational logics" referred to by Routledge and Cumbers 2009:26, 24, 56).

An important argument in this paper is that the ability to connect internationally varies greatly among actors. As others have shown, subalterns are not necessarily "stuck in place" (Featherstone 2007, Hale and Wills 2007), as earlier scale perspectives would assume. However, as the empirical case seems to suggest, the ability of actors to participate in international activities is not unconstrained. It has mainly been individuals in leadership positions in the association that have participated in international activities and women have sometimes been at a disadvantage. This indicates that transnational networks and connectivity within them are not to be taken for granted: they are not "instantaneous", as Featherstone et al. (2007:389) state. The findings caution against assumptions about unrestrained mobility, fluidity, access and inclusiveness inherent in much of the writing on networks. Differential opportunities for participating in international activities suggest that boundaries, while not fixed, continue to be at work in these networks. The paper illustrates how such boundaries are socially constructed and how the maintenance of disconnections requires active work – for example, through gate-keeping practices that exclude or select who to send abroad. These practices are only one set among a wider constellation of cultural, economic and political factors that interact to shape unequal participation in transnational networks – including gender inequalities (Routledge 2008:209, 212). In the studied case, women's relative disadvantage is at least partly related to local gender relations and idioms, thereby confirming arguments that transnational networks are embedded in place-based social relations and cultures rather than deterritorialized (Cumbers et al. 2008, Conway 2008). But the roots of unequal access to networks should not be solely associated with place-based constraints, as they may also be located at others scales.

The understanding of unequal participation in transnational activist networks thus requires an approach that is sensitive to the multiple and unequal spatialities of transnational networks - as the approach proposed in the works of Featherstone and Routledge and his associates. In this respect, some of the insights from the scale literature are worth retaining. In particular, the way in which the ability to "re-scale" is viewed as linked to social power – although not confining this ability to capital and state – is relevant for understanding how women and men in the studied association seem to be differently positioned to participate in international interactions. Scalar practices – in this case, both boundary transgressing and gate-keeping practices – are related to political struggles and may thus have political consequences (Moore 2008). If scale is both the outcome and the medium of struggles for power, and scalar transformations tend to strengthen some actors and disempower others, the differential rescaling described in the paper may have political significance. For example, will existing gender asymmetries in transnational connections result in the empowerment of men in relation to women?

This paper has drawn considerable inspiration from work that problematizes issues of power in transnational networks. The findings lend support to Routledge's (2008) argument that power, while dispersed, is unequally distributed in the network and that actors are differentially "empowered", reflecting differences in mobility, in access to resources and information. He refers to the role of imagineers who tend to have "disproportionate yet productive power" (Routledge 2008:212–3). Furthermore, the difficult realities in which grassroots activists operate in the Global South make them "more dependent upon key nodal points" and imagineers (Cumbers et al. 2008:189, Routledge 2008:213). The case presented in this paper shows how, in the context of extremely limited resources, of restrained mobility and poor access to information technologies in which the Mozambican association exists, participation in the transnational activist network is heavily mediated, rather than direct. Firstly, the leadership of the association controls the flow of information with international partners. In one case, this involved withholding an invitation to the female leader of the women's department. It also included opting for silence, when the association leaders failed to present a written report to international representatives on the contentious exchange visit by the South Africans and failed to provide explanations when they did not send delegates to an international event. In their "translating" role, the (dominantly male) association leaders also seem to have filtered the vision of the network by conveniently omitting the progressive gender policies adopted by the international network. Secondly, as mentioned, the male leaders engaged in gendered gate-keeping, through which they exerted considerable influence over whom to send abroad. This suggests that imagineers, considered by Routledge to be so critical in furthering connectivity, mobilizing the grassroots etc., by virtue of the power ascribed to them by their nodal positions, may sometimes become gate-keepers, agents of disconnection, key actors in the construction of boundaries and involved in the reproduction of power relations.

The identified practices of gendered gate-keeping find some resonance with the exclusionary practices and policing of networks mentioned by Featherstone (2007) in his study of transnational activism against the slave trade in the past. Such practices, he argues, resulted in "largely male and largely white transnational ... networks" (p. 447). As Hawkesworth (2006:11) states, "gender power operates through prohibitions, exclusions ... that circumscribe women's lives" and keep women in place (Pettman 1996). This article uncovers how the spatialities of transnational networks are gendered and suggests that there is much to be gained from looking into the various manifestations of gender inequalities in transnational networks. In this way, the article lends support to a growing critique of gender-blind scholarship on anti-globalization activism and to current calls for a gendering of the politics of transnational resistance (see for example, Marchand 2005; Mohanty 2006). As Conway (2008:18) puts it, we need to inquire "what people ... get to be 'transnational'?" and "to treat representations of the transnational as 'scalar narratives', which authorize some actors ... while minimizing or invisibilizing others".

Acknowledging issues of unequal power and boundary construction in networks also opens up for considering the ways in which such power may be challenged and contested and boundaries subverted – i.e., "the productive dimensions" of power that Routledge (2008:199) argues are absent in many network analyses. In the studied case, tensions and struggles over gender issues emerged at several levels. Exchanges with international partners de-naturalized the gender hierarchy within the association, providing women members with an opportunity to assess that hierarchy and apparently provoking a degree of gender unrest within the association. Exchange visits between member groups in the network served (at least temporarily) to by-pass the power of mediators in the association, by bringing the gender policy of the network to local women members who were unable to travel and were subjected to the filtering practices of the mediators. At the same time, international encounters also generated tensions related to differences in gender ideologies, including issues pertaining to dual-sex organizing and the difficulties the association had in complying with the gender principles of the international network. This resonates with ongoing debates on the adequacy of international feminist norms and models for women's organizing.

Feminist scholars warn against ethnocentric attempts to universalize feminism and against assumptions about sameness "in the forms of women's oppression and women's movements cross-nationally" (Basu 1995:1, 19, Mackie 2001,

Naples 2002a, b). They challenge "the myth of global sisterhood" and universal ideologies of women's liberation and interrogate who has the power and privilege to define what are the legitimate forms of women's struggles. Instead, they highlight the diversity of women's activism and the "profound differences in women's lives and in the meanings of feminism" across the world (Basu 1995:4, Naples 2002a:6). There is increasing awareness that universal feminist worldviews often collide with feminist values and priorities in many local/national contexts (Naples 2002b:275) as well as of the tensions that often emerge between global and local feminisms (Basu 1995, Naples 2002a, Miles 2004). The challenge is thus how to "link diverse local feminisms into transnational solidarities, without universalizing and replicating cultural and economic hegemony" (Mackie 2001:195). This requires a willingness to work with differences (Weber 2002, Miles 2004:11), at all levels, i.e., within and between associations, at the local and at the international level.

Some suggest that it is possible to uphold some basic universal goals and visions concerning, for example, gender equality, while respecting local specificities (Ackerly 2004, Miles 2004:4). This also relates to the discussion on vertical versus horizontal relations in transnational movements and the issue of power. In the case of the international network examined here, the adopted gender policies are to encourage, not dictate, gender equality within member organizations. The stricter quotas for the participation of women in international activities provide an important mechanism for restricting the power of gate-keepers, particularly regarding women. They potentially improve chances for women to take part in international activities, which suggests that such "hierarchical" or vertical directives may actually help to democratize participation. This serves as a caution against dichotomous assumptions that "verticalism is exclusionary and alienating" (Routledge and Cumbers 2009:51) while acephalous horizontal networks are necessarily more democratic and participatory. Since in "ungoverned" horizontal networks, gatekeeping practices would probably go unchecked or unnoticed, potentially leaving women trapped in place, a measure of verticality might be beneficial. Ultimately, however, the verticality or horizontality of relations and their effects must be assessed empirically rather than assumed a priori.

From a scalar perspective, the tensions and struggles arising from the rescaling or transnationalization of the connections of the studied association may well be referred to as a politics of scale, albeit of a different kind from the unidirectional and narrow one associated with earlier notions of scale politics. What emerges is a complex politics that is multidirectional, multi-sited, involving multiple (grassroots) actors and points of interaction. This is a politics that, while not flat in terms of power distribution, involves negotiations along multiple connections that connect actors across sites and places. Such a politics requires the consideration of both spatially extensive and territorially intensive relations, of place-based struggles and their relation to broader networks, of both horizontal and vertical practices. What also comes to light in this paper is the thoroughly gendered nature of this politics.

The spatialities of transnational activist networks such as the one examined in this paper are thus not given or unproblematic. As Featherstone et al. (2007:389) have stated, the *when* and *where* of transnational networks are not to be taken for granted, as such networks are spatially and temporally constituted. The contours and content of such networks are being constantly reconfigured by struggles and negotiations between the various actors and movements. This paper also indicates the need for a socially differentiated understanding of the spatialities of transnational resistance networks – i.e., an understanding that exposes differential abilities to connect along gender, social class and other lines. The article shows that such networks, rather than being accessible to all, are pervaded by exclusions and ruptured by boundaries that are actively constructed and monitored. The powers of mediation at work seem to be of particular importance in contexts where a combination of factors – such as the configuration of local gender relations and widespread material deprivation – keep large sections of the grassroots in place (see also Cumbers et al. 2008:189). But these unequal spatialities of transnational activism may also be characterized by contestation, by struggles for inclusion and by the subverting and transcending of boundaries. Such processes are at the heart of a truly emancipatory politics.

References

Ackerly, B., 2004, "Women's human rights activists as political theorists", in L. Ricciutelli, A. Miles and M. McFadden (eds), *Feminist politics, activism and vision: local and global challenges*. Ontario and London and New York: Inanna Publications and Education Inc. and Zed Books.

Amin, A., 2002, "Spatialities of globalization", *Environment and Planning A*, 34(3):385–99.

—, 2004, "Regions unbound: Towards a new politics of place", *Geografiska Annaler, Series B, Human Geography*, 86(1):33–44.

Amoore, L. (ed.), 2005, *The global resistance reader*. London and New York: Routledge.

Basu, A. (ed.), 1995, *The challenge of local feminisms: women's movements in global perspective*. Boulder and Oxford: Westview Press.

Bayat, A., 2004, "Globalization and the politics of the informals in the Global South", in A. Roy and N. Alsayyad (eds, *Urban Informality: Transnational Perspectives from the Middle East, Latin America, and South Asia*. Lanham: Lexington Books, 79–102.

Batliwala, S., 2002, "Grassroots movements as transnational actors: implications for global civil society", *Voluntas: International Journal of Voluntary and Nonprofit Organizations*, 13(4):393–409.

Brenner, N., 1999, "Globalization as reterritorialization: The rescaling of urban governance in the European Union", *Urban Studies*, 36:431–51.

—, 2001, "The limits to scale? Methodological reflections on scalar structuration", *Progress in Human Geography*, 25(4):591–614.

Bulkeley, H., 2005, "Reconfiguring environmental governance: Towards a politics of scales and networks", *Political Geography*, 24(8):875–902.

Conway, J., 2008, "Geographies of transnational feminisms: The politics of place and scale in the World March of Women", *Social Politics*, doi:10.1093/sp/jxn010, 1–25.

Cox, K., 1997, "Introduction: Globalization and its politics in question", in K. Cox (ed.), *Spaces of globalization: reasserting the power of the local*. New York: Guilford Press.

Cross, J., 2007, "Pirates on the high streets: the street as a site of local resistance to globalization", in J. Cross and A. Morales (eds), *Street entrepreneurs: people, place and politics in local and global perspective*. London: Routledge, 125–43.

Cumbers, A., P. Routledge and C. Nativel, 2008, "The entangled geographies of global justice networks", *Progress in Human Geography*, 32(2):183–201.

Delaney, D. and H. Leitner, 1997, "The political construction of scale", *Political Geography*, 16(2):93–7.

Dirlik, A., 2001, "Place-based imagination: globalism and the politics of place", in R. Prazniak, and A. Dirlik (eds), *Places and politics in an age of globalization*. New York and Oxford: Rowman & Littlefield.

Escobar, A., 2001, "Culture sits in places: Reflections on globalism and subaltern strategies of localization", *Political Geography*, 20:139–74.

Featherstone, D., 2003, "Spatialities of transnational resistance to globalization: The maps of grievance of the Inter-Continental Caravan", *Transactions of the Institute of British Geographers*, 28:404–21.

—, 2004, "Spatial relations and the materialities of political conflict: The construction of entangled political identities in the London and Newcastle Port Strikes of 1768", *Geoforum*, 35(6):701–11.

—, 2007, "The spatial politics of the past unbound: Transnational networks and the making of political identities", *Global Networks*, 7(4):430–52.

—, 2008, *Resistance, space and political identities: the making of counter-global networks*. Sussex, Oxford and Malden: Wiley-Blackwell.

—, R. Phillips and J. Waters, 2007, "Introduction: Spatialities of transnational networks", *Global Networks*, 7(4):383–91.

Gibson-Graham, J., 2002, "Beyond global vs. local: economic politics outside the binary frame", in A. Herod, and M. Wright (eds), *Geographies of power: placing scale*. Malden, Oxford, Victoria and Berlin: Blackwell.

Gough, J., 2004, "Changing scale as changing class relations: Variety and contradiction in the politics of scale", *Political Geography*, 23:185–211.

Hale, A. and J. Wills, 2007, "Women Working Worldwide: Transnational networks, corporate social responsibility and action research", *Global Networks*, 7(4):453–76.

Hardt, M. and A. Negri, 2001, *Empire*. Cambridge: Harvard University Press.

—, 2004, *Multitude: war and democracy in the age of empire*. Cambridge: Harvard University Press.

Hawkesworth, M., 2006, *Globalization and feminist activism*. Lanham, Boulder, New York, Toronto and Oxford: Rowman & Littlefield.

Herod, A. and M. Wright, 2002, "Placing scale: an introduction", in A. Herod and M. Wright (eds), *Geographies of power: placing scale*. Malden, Oxford, Victoria and Berlin: Blackwell.

Howitt, R., 2003, "Scale", in J. Agnew, K. Mitchell and G. Toal (eds), *A companion to political geography*. Oxford: Blackwell.

Juris, J.S., 2004, "Networked social movements: global movements for global justice", in M. Castells (ed.), *The network society: a cross-cultural perspective*. Cheltenham: Edward Edgar.

Lachartre, B., 2000, *Enjeux urbains au Mozambique: de Lourenço Marques à Maputo*. Paris: Éditions Karthala.

Lindell, I., 2008, "The multiple sites of urban governance: Insights from an African city", *Urban Studies*, 45(10):1879–1901.

—, (ed.), 2010, *Africa's Informal workers: collective agency, alliances and transnational organizing in urban Africa*. London and Uppsala: Zed Books and The Nordic Africa Institute.

Lundin, I. , 2001, *Reflections on the dynamics of a nation building process under stress: the case of Mozambique 1993–1998,* Choros 2001:2, Göteborg: Kulturgeografiska institutionen, Handelshögskolan vid Göteborgs Universitet.

Lyons, L., 2004, "Organizing for domestic worker rights in Singapore: the limits of transnationalism", in L. Ricciutelli, A. Miles and M. McFadden (eds), *Feminist politics, activism and vision: local and global challenges.* Ontario and London and New York: Inanna Publications and Education Inc. and Zed Books.

Mackie, V., 2001, "The language of globalization, transnationality and feminism", *International Feminist Journal of Politics,* 3(2):180–206.

Marchand, M., 2005, "Some theoretical "musings" about gender and resistance", in L. Amoore (ed.), *The global resistance reader.*London and New York: Routledge, 215–25.

Marston, S., J.P. Jones and K. Woodward, 2005, "Human geography without scale", *Transactions of the Institute of British Geographers,* 30(4):416–32.

Massey, D., 1993, "Power-geometry and a progressive sense of place", in J. Bird, B. Curtis, T. Putnam and G. Robertson (eds), *Mapping the futures: local cultures, global change.* London and New York: Routledge.

—, 1999, "Imagining globalization: power-geometries of time-space", in D. Massey (ed.), *Power-geometries and the politics of space-time,* Hettner-Lectures 2, University of Heidelberg, Heidelberg.

—, 2004, "Geographies of responsibility", *Geografiska Annaler,* Series B, Human Geography, 86B(1):5–18.

Masson, D., 2006, "Constructing scale/contesting scale: Women's movement and rescaling politics in Quebec", *Social Politics,* 13(4):462–86.

McDowell, L., 2001, "Linking scales: or how research about gender and organizations raises new issues for economic geography", *Journal of Economic Geography,* 1:227–250.

Mendez, J., 2002, "Creating alternatives from a gender perspective: transnational organizing for maquila workers' rights in Central America", in N. Naples and M. Desai (eds) *Women's activism and globalization: linking local struggles and transnational politics.* New York and London: Routledge.

Miles, A., 2004, "Introduction", in L. Ricciutelli, A. Miles and M. McFadden (eds), *Feminist politics, activism and vision: local and global challenges.* Ontario and London and New York: Inanna Publications and Education Inc. and Zed Books.

Mohanty, C. ,2006, *Feminism without borders: decolonizing theory, practicing solidarity.* Durham and London: Duke University Press.

Moore, A., 2008, "Rethinking scale as a geographical category: From analysis to practice", *Progress in Human Geography,* 32(2):203–225.

Naples, N., 2002a, "Changing the terms: community activism, globalization, and the dilemmas of transnational feminist praxis", in N. Naples and M. Desai (eds), *Women's activism and globalization: linking local struggles and transnational politics.* New York and London: Routledge.

—, 2002b, "The challenges and possibilities of transnational feminist praxis", in N. Naples and M. Desai (eds), *Women's activism and globalization: linking local struggles and transnational politics*. New York and London: Routledge.

Peterson, V. and A. Runyan , 2005, "The politics of resistance: women as nonstate, antistate and transstate actors", in L. Amoore (ed.), *The global resistance reader*. London and New York: Routledge, 226–43.

Pettman, J., 1996, *Worlding women*. London: Routledge.

Ricciutelli, L., A. Miles and M. McFadden (eds), 2004, *Feminist politics, activism and vision: local and global challenges*. Ontario and London and New York: Inanna Publications and Education Inc. and Zed Books.

Routledge, P., 2003, "Convergence space: Process geographies of grassroots globalization networks", *Transactions of the Institute of British Geographers, 28:333–49.

—, 2008, "Acting in the network: ANT and the politics of generating associations", *Environment and Planning D*, 26:199–217.

—, and A. Cumbers, 2009, *Global justice networks: geographies of transnational solidarity*. Manchester and New York: Manchester University Press.

Sidaway, J., 2007, "Commentary: Negotiating the spatialities of transnational networks", *Global Networks*, 7:498–501.

Smith, N., 1992, "Geography, difference and the politics of scale", in J. Doherty, E. Graham and M. Malek (eds), *Postmodernism and the social sciences*. Basingstoke: Macmillan.

—, 1993, "Homeless/global: scaling places", in J. Bird, B. Curtis, T. Putnam, G. Robertson and L. Tickner (eds), *Mapping the futures: local cultures, global change*. London and New York: Routledge.

Swyngedouw, E., 1997, "Neither global nor local: 'glocalization' and the politics of scale", in K. Cox (ed.), *Spaces of globalization: reasserting the power of the local*. New York: Guilford Press.

—, 2000, "Authoritarian governance, power and the politics of rescaling", *Environment and Planning D: Society and Space*, 18:63–76.

Tamale, S., 2004, "Alternative leadership in Africa: some critical feminist reflections", in L. Ricciutelli, A. Miles and M. McFadden (eds), *Feminist politics, activism and vision: local and global challenges*. Ontario and London and New York: Inanna Publications and Education Inc. and Zed Books.

Uitermark, J., 2002, "Re-scaling, 'scale fragmentation' and the regulation of antagonistic relationships", *Progress in Human Geography*, 26(6):743–65.

Weber, C., 2002, "Women to women: dissident citizen diplomacy in Nicaragua", in N. Naples and M. Desai (eds), *Women's activism and globalization: linking local struggles and transnational politics*. New York and London: Routledge.

CURRENT AFRICAN ISSUES PUBLISHED BY THE INSTITUTE

Recent issues in the series are available electronically
for download free of charge www.nai.uu.se

1. *South Africa, the West and the Frontline States. Report from a Seminar.* 1981, 34 pp, (out-of print)

2. Maja Naur, *Social and Organisational Change in Libya.* 1982, 33 pp, (out-of print)

3. *Peasants and Agricultural Production in Africa. A Nordic Research Seminar. Follow-up Reports and Discussions.* 1981, 34 pp, (out-of print)

4. Ray Bush & S. Kibble, *Destabilisation in Southern Africa, an Overview.* 1985, 48 pp, (out-of print)

5. Bertil Egerö, *Mozambique and the Southern African Struggle for Liberation.* 1985, 29 pp, (out-of print)

6. Carol B. Thompson, *Regional Economic Polic under Crisis Condition. Southern African Development.* 1986, 34 pp, (out-of print)

7. Inge Tvedten, *The War in Angola, Internal Conditions for Peace and Recovery.* 1989, 14 pp, (out-of print)

8. Patrick Wilmot, *Nigeria's Southern Africa Policy 1960–1988.* 1989, 15 pp, (out-of print)

9. Jonathan Baker, *Perestroika for Ethiopia: In Search of the End of the Rainbow?* 1990, 21 pp, (out-of print)

10. Horace Campbell, *The Siege of Cuito Cuanavale.* 1990, 35 pp, (out-of print)

11. Maria Bongartz, *The Civil War in Somalia. Its genesis and dynamics.* 1991, 26 pp, (out-of print)

12. Shadrack B.O. Gutto, *Human and People's Rights in Africa. Myths, Realities and Prospects.* 1991, 26 pp, (out-of print)

13. Said Chikhi, Algeria. *From Mass Rebellion to Workers' Protest.* 1991, 23 pp, (out-of print)

14. Bertil Odén, *Namibia's Economic Links to South Africa.* 1991, 43 pp, (out-of print)

15. Cervenka Zdenek, *African National Congress Meets Eastern Europe. A Dialogue on Common Experiences.* 1992, 49 pp, ISBN 91-7106-337-4, (out-of print)

16. Diallo Garba, *Mauritania–The Other Apartheid?* 1993, 75 pp, ISBN 91-7106-339-0, (out-of print)

17. Zdenek Cervenka and Colin Legum, *Can National Dialogue Break the Power of Terror in Burundi?* 1994, 30 pp, ISBN 91-7106-353-6, (out-of print)

18. Erik Nordberg and Uno Winblad, *Urban Environmental Health and Hygiene in Sub- Saharan Africa.* 1994, 26 pp, ISBN 91-7106-364-1, (out-of print)

19. Chris Dunton and Mai Palmberg, *Human Rights and Homosexuality in Southern Africa.* 1996, 48 pp, ISBN 91-7106-402-8, (out-of print)

20. Georges Nzongola-Ntalaja *From Zaire to the Democratic Republic of the Congo.* 1998, 18 pp, ISBN 91-7106-424-9, (out-of print)

21. Filip Reyntjens, *Talking or Fighting? Political Evolution in Rwanda and Burundi, 1998–1999.* 1999, 27 pp, ISBN 91-7106-454-0, SEK 80.-

22. Herbert Weiss, *War and Peace in the Democratic Republic of the Congo.* 1999, 28 pp, ISBN 91-7106-458-3, SEK 80,-

23. Filip Reyntjens, *Small States in an Unstable Region – Rwanda and Burundi, 1999–2000,* 2000, 24 pp, ISBN 91-7106-463-X, (out-of print)

24. Filip Reyntjens, *Again at the Crossroads: Rwanda and Burundi, 2000–2001.* 2001, 25 pp, ISBN 91-7106-483-4, (out-of print)

25. Henning Melber, *The New African Initiative and the African Union. A Preliminary Assessment and Documentation.* 2001, 36 pp, ISBN 91-7106-486-9, (out-of print)

26. Dahilon Yassin Mohamoda, *Nile Basin Cooperation. A Review of the Literature.* 2003, 39 pp, ISBN 91-7106-512-1, SEK 90,-

27. Henning Melber (ed.), *Media, Public Discourse and Political Contestation in Zimbabwe.* 2004, 39 pp, ISBN 91-7106-534-2, SEK 90,-

28. Georges Nzongola-Ntalaja, *From Zaire to the Democratic Republic of the Congo.* Second and Revised Edition. 2004, 23 pp, ISBN-91-7106-538-5, (out-of print)

29. Henning Melber (ed.), *Trade, Development, Cooperation – What Future for Africa?* 2005, 44 pp, ISBN 91-7106-544-X, SEK 90,-

30. Kaniye S.A. Ebeku, *The Succession of Faure Gnassingbe to the Togolese Presidency – An International Law Perspective.* 2005, 32 pp, ISBN 91-7106-554-7, SEK 90,-

31. Jeffrey V. Lazarus, Catrine Christiansen, Lise Rosendal Østergaard, Lisa Ann Richey, *Models for Life – Advancing antiretroviral therapy in sub-Saharan Africa.* 2005, 33 pp, ISBN 91-7106-556-3, SEK 90,-

32. Charles Manga Fombad and Zein Kebonang, *AU, NEPAD and the APRM – Democratisation Efforts Explored.* Edited by Henning Melber. 2006, 56 pp, ISBN 91-7106-569-5, SEK 90,-

33. Pedro Pinto Leite, Claes Olsson, Magnus Schöldtz, Toby Shelley, Pål Wrange, Hans Corell and Karin Scheele, *The Western Sahara Conflict – The Role of Natural Resources in Decolonization.* Edited by Claes Olsson. 2006, 32 pp, ISBN 91-7106-571-7, SEK 90,-

34. Jassey, Katja and Stella Nyanzi, *How to Be a "Proper" Woman in the Times of HIV and AIDS.* 2007, 35 pp, ISBN 91-7106-574-1, SEK 90,-

35. Lee, Margaret, Henning Melber, Sanusha Naidu and Ian Taylor, *China in Africa.* Compiled by Henning Melber. 2007, 47 pp, ISBN 978-91-7106-589-6, SEK 90,-

36. Nathaniel King, *Conflict as Integration. Youth Aspiration to Personhood in the Teleology of Sierra Leone's 'Senseless War'.* 2007, 32 pp, ISBN 978-91-7106-604-6, SEK 90,-

37. Aderanti Adepoju, *Migration in sub-Saharan Africa.* 2008. 70 pp, ISBN 978-91-7106-620-6, SEK 110,-

38. Bo Malmberg, *Demography and the development potential of sub-Saharan Africa.* 2008, 39 pp, 978-91-7106-621-3

39. Johan Holmberg, *Natural resources in sub-Saharan Africa: Assets and vulnerabilities.* 2008, 52 pp, 978-91-7106-624-4

40. Arne Bigsten and Dick Durevall, *The African economy and its role in the world economy.* 2008, 66 pp, 978-91-7106-625-1

41. Fantu Cheru, *Africa's development in the 21st century: Reshaping the research agenda.* 2008, 47 pp, 978-91-7106-628-2

42. Dan Kuwali, Persuasive Prevention. *Towards a Principle for Implementing Article 4(h) and R2P by the African Union.* 2009. 70 pp. ISBN 978-91-7106-650-3

43. Daniel Volman, *China, India, Russia and the United States. The Scramble for African Oil and the Militarization of the Continent.* 2009. 24 pp. ISBN 978-91-7106-658-9

44. Mats Hårsmar, *Understanding Poverty in Africa? A Navigation through Disputed Concepts, Data and Terrains.* 2010. 54 pp. ISBN 978-91-7106-668-8

45. Sam Maghimbi, Razack B. Lokina and Mathew A. Senga, *The Agrarian Question in Tanzania? A State of the Art Paper.* 2011. 67 pp. ISBN 978-91-7106-684-8

46. William Minter, *African Migration, Global Inequalities, and Human Rights. Connecting the Dots.* 2011. 95 pp. ISBN 978-91-7106-692-3

47. Musa Abutudu and Dauda Garuba, *Natural Resource Governance and Eiti Implementation in Nigeria.* 2011. 74 pp. ISBN 978-91-7106-708-1

48. Ilda Lindell, *Transnational Activism Networks and Gendered Gatekeeping. Negotiating Gender in an African Association of Informal Workers.*
2011. 44 pp. ISBN 978-91-7106-712-8

www.ingramcontent.com/pod-product-compliance
Lightning Source LLC
LaVergne TN
LVHW061303060426
835510LV00014B/1859